CW01072510

Original title:
The Feeling Tree

Author: Theodore Sinclair
ISBN HARDBACK: 978-9916-88-926-8
ISBN PAPERBACK: 978-9916-88-927-5

Revelations in the Twilight

In twilight's glow, the shadows creep,
Whispers of secrets, they softly leap.
Stars blink awake in the fading light,
Promising wonders, a mystical sight.

Through the breeze, the soft sighs play,
Nature's breath at the close of day.
Leaves murmur tales of the moon's ascent,
As twilight speaks, the world is bent.

Colors blend in a dusky sea,
Hints of magic, wild and free.
Time stands still as the day takes flight,
In this tender dance of day and night.

Hold your heart, let the moment last,
Each revelation, a bridge to the past.
In twilight's arms, dreams intertwine,
A sacred space where the stars align.

Swaying with Secrets

In the whispering winds so soft,
Leaves dance high, secrets aloft.
Shadows hide, stories untold,
Nature's voice, ancient and bold.

Beneath the boughs where stillness reigns,
Hidden truths in nature's chains.
Each rustle speaks with gentle ease,
Inviting hearts to find their peace.

Essence of Existence

In every breath, a fleeting spark,
Moments weave in the quiet dark.
Stars above whisper of time,
Life's melody, a flowing rhyme.

With every dawn, hope takes flight,
Painting skies with colors bright.
Holding dreams in fragile hands,
A journey mapped in shifting sands.

Vines of Vulnerability

Tender shoots that intertwine,
Cloaked in shadows, they define.
Reaching out, they crave the sun,
A dance of trust, two become one.

In each embrace, a story grows,
Through the thorns, beauty flows.
Fragile hearts, though worn and torn,
In vulnerability, love is born.

Serene Interludes

Calm waters reflect the sky,
Moments pause, the world goes by.
In silent whispers, peace unfolds,
Time slows down, the heart beholds.

Golden rays through branches peek,
In nature's arms, we softly speak.
Finding solace in each embrace,
In serene interludes, we find grace.

Ripples in the Light

Gentle waves caress the shore,
Sunlight glimmers, evermore.
Whispers dance on soft, warm sand,
Nature's grace at our command.

Each ripple tells a tale anew,
Mirrored skies in vibrant hue.
Breezes carry dreams untold,
In this moment, life unfolds.

A Garden of Souls

Beneath the boughs where shadows play,
Laughter blooms in bright array.
Petals whisper secrets near,
In this sanctuary, we revere.

Every flower holds a dream,
Rustling softly, they will gleam.
Nurtured by the hands of time,
In this space, our spirits climb.

Dancing Shadows

In twilight's glow, figures sway,
Chasing dusk, they slip away.
Flickering dreams in silver night,
Every turn reveals delight.

With every step, the stories weave,
Of love and loss, we dare believe.
Shadows swirl, a fleeting glance,
Carried forth in twilight's dance.

Touched by the Breeze

A whisper from the trees above,
Brings a feeling like a hug.
Gentle hands that softly trace,
Nature's breath, a warm embrace.

Leaves flutter with each subtle sigh,
As wild hearts learn to fly.
In every gust, a promise found,
In this moment, we are bound.

Flickers of Hope

In shadows deep where silence lies,
A glimmer fights, unyielding skies.
With every breath, the spirit soars,
Each whisper kind, the heart restores.

The night will fade, the dawn will break,
In cracks of hope, the brave awake.
For in the dark, a spark ignites,
A promise found, a soul's delights.

Nestled in Nature

Among the trees, where whispers blend,
The gentle breeze, a timeless friend.
Soft petals fall on a quiet stream,
In nature's heart, we find our dream.

The rustling leaves, a calming song,
In every shade, we all belong.
With every step on this green ground,
In nature's arms, our peace is found.

The Warmth of Shelter

Beneath a roof, where love resides,
The laughter sings, the fear subsides.
With open arms, the hearth glows bright,
In cozy nooks, we find our light.

The world outside may storm and rage,
But here we turn a loving page.
The warmth we share, a treasure rare,
In every heart, we touch and care.

Boundless Horizons

Beyond the hills, the skies so vast,
A journey calls, we rise up fast.
With every step, new dreams unfold,
The world awaits, in hues of gold.

The open road, a promise near,
Each moment lived, we hold so dear.
With courage found, we break the chains,
To chase the light that ever reigns.

Canopy of Yearning

Beneath the trees we often stand,
Searching for a touch, a hand.
Whispered winds through leaves above,
Speak the secrets of our love.

Stars emerge in twilight's glow,
Guiding hearts where rivers flow.
In the night, dreams come alive,
In this space, our souls will thrive.

Shades of Affection

In the garden where we play,
Colors blend in soft array.
Petals whisper soft and sweet,
Heartbeats dance, where lovers meet.

Through the dusk, our shadows blend,
In this warmth, our spirits mend.
Hand in hand, we burn so bright,
Painting stars upon the night.

The Language of Sap

Deep within the ancient trees,
Life flows with the gentle breeze.
In each drop, a story's spun,
Of the moon, the earth, the sun.

Roots entwined beneath the ground,
In silence, wisdom's found.
Layers tell of years gone past,
Echoes of the shadows cast.

Blossom of Dreams

In the dawn, the flowers wake,
Every petal, a promise we make.
Sunlight dances on their face,
Whispers of a sweet embrace.

With each bloom, our hopes ascend,
In the garden, love won't end.
Together in this radiant space,
We find strength, we find grace.

Tapestry of Emotions

Threads of joy weave bright and bold,
Whispers of sorrow in stories told.
Colors blend in a dance so sweet,
Hearts entwined where dreams and fears meet.

Laughter echoes through the air,
Tears like jewels, both light and rare.
Joy and pain, a beautiful mix,
Life's rich tapestry, the heart's fix.

In the silence, feelings reside,
Comfort found where love's confide.
Moments fleeting, yet they stay,
In the tapestry, they'll never fray.

The Echo of Bark

In the hush of the twilight glare,
Whispers of secrets fill the air.
Ancient trees stand tall and wise,
With tales that echo beneath the skies.

Bark etched deep with the scars of time,
Stories captured in rhythm and rhyme.
Each ring a memory, each crack a sigh,
In the forest's heart, where shadows lie.

Creatures scurry, life unfolds,
Underneath the canopy's gold.
Nature's choir sings soft and clear,
In the echo of bark, the world we hear.

Cry of the Sapling

In the cradle of Earth, a sapling sows,
Reaching for sunlight as the cool breeze blows.
Tender and new, with leaves so bright,
Whispering dreams to the stars at night.

Roots struggling deep, yet growing strong,
In a world that can feel so wrong.
Each drop of rain a lesson learned,
And in every storm, resilience burned.

The cry of a sapling, a voice so pure,
Yearning for growth, a quest to endure.
Through shadows and doubts, it finds its way,
A symbol of hope in the light of day.

Autumn's Embrace

Crimson leaves fall like whispered dreams,
Nature awakens with soft, golden beams.
The air turns crisp, a sweet perfume,
As seasons shift, and change finds room.

Harvest moon rises, glowing bright,
Bringing warmth to the cool of night.
In every branch, a story unfolds,
Of love and loss, as time gently molds.

In the stillness, peace can be found,
Amidst the vibrant, painted ground.
Autumn's embrace, a tender farewell,
In its silence, the heart can dwell.

The Language of Leaves

In whispers green, they dance and sway,
Beneath the sun, they find their play.
Each flutter soft, a tale they weave,
In rustling tones, they softly grieve.

Through summer's breath, they share their dreams,
Through autumn's glow, a burst of schemes.
In winter's hush, they stand so bare,
Yet springtime brings new life to share.

Seasons of Sentiment

In springtime's light, we start anew,
With petals bright and skies so blue.
Summer's warmth ignites our hearts,
As laughter flows and joy imparts.

Autumn whispers, gold and red,
Memories of what we once said.
Winter wraps us, cold and still,
Yet love persists, a warming thrill.

Harmony in Hibernation

In silence deep, the world takes pause,
Nature sleeps, without a cause.
A blanket white, the earth's embrace,
In quietude, we find our place.

The stars above, they twinkle bright,
Guiding dreams through endless night.
In stillness borne, the heart finds peace,
In hibernation, worries cease.

A Symphony of Shades

In twilight hues, the colors blend,
A canvas wide, where dreams transcend.
Each shadow cast tells tales untold,
In every shade, a spark of gold.

From dawn's first blush to dusk's farewell,
A melody in each tone we dwell.
In nature's brush, our spirits soar,
A symphony sung forevermore.

Canopy of Connections

Under the leaves, we gather tight,
Threads of friendship, woven bright.
Whispers of secrets in soft green hues,
The bonds we share, forever renew.

Branches embracing, stories unfold,
Memories cherished, treasures untold.
In nature's arms, hearts intertwine,
Beneath the canopy, our souls align.

Sunlight dances through the trees,
Carrying laughter on gentle breeze.
Together we thrive, nurturing the ground,
In this sacred space, love is found.

Leaves may fall, but roots run deep,
In the heart of the forest, friendships keep.
A sheltering world, a quiet retreat,
In this canopy of connections, we meet.

Sap of Serenity

In tranquil mornings, dew drops cling,
Nature whispers, a gentle spring.
With every breath, the stillness grows,
In the heart's corners, peace bestows.

Beneath the bark, life flows unseen,
Rich with wisdom, setting the scene.
Branches reach out, to touch the sky,
In every heartbeat, the spirit sighs.

Clouds drift softly, casting their shade,
Where whispers of calm and solace parade.
The world slows down, in moments vast,
As the sap of serenity holds fast.

In stillness found, we learn to share,
The quiet strength that lingers there.
Nature's embrace, a soothing balm,
In its presence, we find our calm.

Dance of the Wind

Rippling whispers through the trees,
The wind weaves tales with effortless ease.
Leaves twirl lightly, a ballet grand,
Nature's chorus in perfect band.

From mountain tops to valleys low,
A dance unfolds, a graceful flow.
Fingers of breeze tease with delight,
Guiding dreams into moonlit night.

Songs of the earth on wings take flight,
Chasing shadows that drift from sight.
In every gust, a story unfurls,
The universe spins, as magic swirls.

With every sigh, the world does sway,
In the dance of the wind, we find our way.
A symphony played on nature's stage,
Flowing together, age to age.

Echoing Laughter

In valleys deep, with voices clear,
Laughter rings out, drawing near.
A symphony sweet, in echoes lost,
In the heart's joy, we count the cost.

Moments shared, like ripples arise,
In each chuckle, the spirit flies.
Memories linger, in playful tone,
The warmth of friendship brightly shone.

Through open fields, the echoes roam,
In every heart, they find a home.
Light as feathers, soaring high,
In the tapestry of life, we fly.

As twilight falls, the laughter stays,
In glowing embers, the warmth conveys.
In every heart, a story spun,
Echoing laughter, forever fun.

Branches of Heartstrings

In the quiet dusk of evening light,
Branches sway, hearts take flight.
Dreams entwined in whispers soft,
Yearning souls, to love, we oft.

Beneath the canopy, secrets breathe,
Bound by feelings, we both believe.
Nature's pulse, a gentle guide,
In the rustling leaves, our hopes reside.

When storms may rage, and shadows loom,
Together, we find a brightened room.
Each branch that bends, a tale unfolds,
Of heartstrings woven, a treasure untold.

As twilight fades, our laughter rings,
In the heart of night, the joy it brings.
Connected still, through years that flow,
Branches and hearts in the soft moon's glow.

Blossoms of Longing

Petals dance in the summer breeze,
Whispers linger, like gentle pleas.
Every bloom, a silent sigh,
In gardens where our dreams lie.

Underneath the azure sky,
Longing lingers, time slips by.
With every glance, a spark ignites,
In the twilight of our nights.

Each flower's hue tells stories grand,
Of sweet encounters, a tender hand.
Fingers trace the softest hues,
Blossoms speak the love we choose.

As dusk transforms the day anew,
In the twilight, I wait for you.
With blossoms bright, our hopes entwine,
In the garden where our hearts align.

Shadows of Solitude

In the stillness, shadows grow,
Solitude wraps, a gentle glow.
Whispers echo through the night,
Loneliness, a fleeting fright.

Beneath the stars, a quiet muse,
Thoughts drifting, they intertwine and fuse.
In shadows cast by the moon's grace,
I find a still and sacred space.

Each heartbeat speaks in muted tones,
Embracing silence, I find my own.
In solitude, a friend I meet,
In every pause, my thoughts repeat.

As dawn approaches, shadows fade,
Yet in solitude, I am remade.
With every breath, the light will flow,
In shadows deep, I've learned to grow.

Echoes in the Canopy

Underneath the leafy dome,
Echoes whisper, far from home.
Branches sway in soft refrain,
Carrying songs of joy and pain.

In the rustling, stories weave,
Ancient tales that hearts believe.
Every rustle, a sigh of fate,
In this canopy, I wait.

Sunlight filters through the green,
The beauty here, gently seen.
Echoes dance on gentle air,
Nature's voice, beyond compare.

As shadows stretch and daylight wanes,
In the stillness, my heart gains.
With every echo, life resounds,
In the canopy, love abounds.

The Dance of the Branches

In the whisper of the breeze, they sway,
Reaching high, then low, in playful display.
Sunlight filtering through their grasping hands,
Nature's song flows in soft, fleeting strands.

Beneath the canopy, shadows intertwine,
With gentle rustles, a secret divine.
A ballet of colors—green, gold, and brown,
A symphony played by trees in their gown.

Growth Amidst Storms

From cracks in the earth, green shoots arise,
Defying the darkness, they rise toward the skies.
With roots that anchor through tempest and rain,
Resilience flourishes despite every pain.

Each drop that falls, a lesson to learn,
In the heart of the storm, there's always a turn.
Petals unfurl, washed clean by the skies,
Forging a path where the brave spirit flies.

Echoes in the Grove

In the hush of the grove, whispers take flight,
Carried by breezes, they dance in the light.
Old roots hold stories of times long ago,
Echoes of laughter, joy, grief, and woe.

Beneath the strong boughs, secrets reside,
In the crook of the branches, time cannot hide.
A tapestry woven with memory's thread,
In the silence of twilight, the past has been said.

Luminescence of Longing

Stars flicker softly in the deep velvet night,
Yearning for moments imbued with pure light.
Each dream that we harbor, a beacon that glows,
Illuminating paths that the heart truly knows.

With each gentle pulse, hope dances and sways,
Through shadows and trials, it steers all our ways.
For in every heartbeat, a promise, a song,
We find luminescence where we all belong.

Leaves of Loneliness

In the whisper of the trees,
Leaves flutter down with ease.
Each one drifts from branch to ground,
A silence where love's lost sound.

Shadows stretch and linger long,
In the twilight, a fading song.
Crimson, gold in the fading light,
Echoes of a once-bright night.

Underneath the whispering sigh,
Hope clings on, though it might die.
Rustling through the empty paths,
Memory holds, through silent laughs.

Yet the roots remain so deep,
In the soil, secrets keep.
For every leaf that turns to dust,
New ones sprout, as in they must.

Fruits of Joyful Sorrow

In the garden of the heart,
Buds bloom near and far apart.
Each petal holds a tale unfurled,
Of joy and pain in intertwined world.

Ripened fruits hang low and bright,
Sweet with laughter, sown in light.
Yet beneath the juicy skin,
Lies the bitter touch within.

Harvest dreams with gentle hands,
Taste the sorrow that life demands.
For in every drop of rain,
Lives a quiet, joyful pain.

So gather close these heartfelt seeds,
In the sorrow, joy proceeds.
Life's paradox in each embrace,
Fruits of sorrow, joy we trace.

Bark of Resilience

Amidst the storm, the trees stand tall,
Bark embracing winds that call.
Textures rough, yet spirit bright,
Holding firm through darkest night.

Each ring whispers tales of years,
Weathered storms and all their fears.
Yet strength flows in every vein,
Life insists, despite the pain.

Rooted deep in sacred ground,
In silence, wisdom can be found.
Through seasons harsh, it holds the flame,
In nature's dance, it plays a game.

So when the world feels cold and stark,
Remember trees with their strong bark.
For in each scar and wrinkle laid,
Resilience blooms, and hope's displayed.

Petals of Dreams

In gardens where the soft winds play,
Petals drift and gently sway.
Colors weave in a fragrant dance,
Each one tells a whispered chance.

Caught in sunlight's golden thread,
Hopes take flight, where fears have fled.
Softly resting on the ground,
Dreams, like flowers, can be found.

In the dew of morning's sheen,
Fragile beauty, rarely seen.
Yet in each bloom, a spark ignites,
Guiding souls through starry nights.

So lift your gaze, embrace the bright,
Petals swirling, a wondrous sight.
For every dream that starts to fade,
Brings forth love, a serenade.

Spiritual Roots

In silence deep, we seek the truth,
A whisper felt in every youth.
Beneath the soil, the ancients lie,
Connecting hearts beyond the sky.

Each breath a prayer, a gentle song,
To roots that hold us all along.
In every tree, a tale unfolds,
In sacred earth, our spirit holds.

With branches wide, we reach for light,
In unity, we find our might.
The journey shared, a sacred bond,
Through spiritual roots, we respond.

Fronds of Memory

In twilight's glow, the past awakes,
A dance of fronds, the heart remakes.
Each leaf a story, whispered low,
As time flows softly, memories grow.

In gentle breezes, secrets sway,
Amongst the fronds, we find our way.
Where laughter lingers, shadows play,
The echoes of those gone astray.

With every sigh, the heart will keep,
The fronds of memory, so deep.
Forever cherished, never lost,
In nature's arms, we count the cost.

Harvest of Hope

Beneath the sun, the seeds are sown,
With care and love, the garden's grown.
Each bud that blooms, a promise bright,
A harvest rich, in morning light.

In fields of gold, we gather dreams,
Amidst the toil, the future gleams.
With every grain, a story told,
Of hope reborn, of hearts consoled.

In shared abundance, strength is found,
With open hands, our joy unbound.
The harvest of hope, forever flows,
In balance with all that nature knows.

Petals and Shadows

In gardens lush, where sunlight plays,
Petals bloom bright through summer days.
Yet shadows linger, gentle gaze,
In nature's dance, a soft malaise.

Each petal's grace, a fleeting wisp,
In moments caught, we grasp and sip.
The shadows tell of stories past,
In quiet corners, memories cast.

Together they weave, a tapestry,
Of love and loss, of what could be.
In petals and shadows, life does flow,
A bittersweet song we come to know.

Roots of Reminiscence

In shadows soft, the memories lie,
Whispers of time that gently sigh.
Branches stretch to skies once blue,
Holding dreams that still feel true.

A dance of leaves in autumn's grace,
Each moment held, a warm embrace.
Echoes linger in the air,
Stories woven, rich and rare.

With every root that grips the earth,
A tale is told of love and worth.
The past, a garden still in bloom,
In quiet corners, it finds room.

As seasons change and rivers flow,
The roots remain, a steady glow.
Anchoring hearts to times once grand,
Nurturing life in this vast land.

Shelter from the Storm

Beneath the roof, the raindrops fall,
We gather close, one and all.
Wind howls fierce, but we stand strong,
In this embrace, we belong.

The tempest rages outside our door,
Yet peace resides forevermore.
Stories shared on weary nights,
Hearts ignite with flickering lights.

Our laughter echoes, a soothing balm,
In the chaos, we discover calm.
Together here, the world seems bright,
A haven born from love's pure light.

As thunder rolls and shadows creep,
In this shelter, dreams we keep.
Hand in hand, we courageously cope,
In unity, we find our hope.

Tides of Transformation

Waves that crash on shores of time,
Shifting sands, a silent rhyme.
With every cycle, change descends,
In nature's dance, the spirit mends.

A seed begins beneath the ground,
In darkness, roots are tightly wound.
When sun breaks forth and rains caress,
The bloom awakens, fresh andBlessed.

The moon reflects on waters deep,
In gentle rhythms, secrets keep.
As seasons ebb, the heart will find,
The call to grow, to redefine.

Embrace the shift, the vast unknown,
For through the tides, we are shown.
Life's precious flow, both bold and bright,
In transformation, we find our light.

The Gravity of Joy

In laughter's lift, we soar so high,
A moment caught, a spark in the sky.
With hearts that race and eyes that shine,
Joy's gentle pull, a sacred sign.

Through simple acts, the world expands,
With every touch, connection stands.
In shared delights, the weight is light,
A gravity that feels so right.

The magic glows in fleeting times,
In whispered words, in joyful chimes.
We dance like leaves in autumn's breeze,
With joy that flows, we find our ease.

So let us gather, let us play,
In the gravity of joy, we stay.
For in each laugh, we touch the divine,
An endless bond, forever entwined.

Seasons of Solitude

In winter's grasp, all is still,
The world outside, so cold and shrill.
Yet in the silence, whispers grow,
A hidden warmth, a gentle glow.

Spring arrives with softer light,
Awakening dreams that took to flight.
Blossoms burst in vibrant hue,
Reviving hope, a promise new.

Summer sings with laughter's ease,
Golden days beneath the trees.
But shadows linger, fears unfold,
In sunny warmth, the heart feels cold.

Autumn's sigh, a bittersweet,
Leaves falling down, a slow retreat.
In every layer, memories blend,
Seasons change, but solitude's a friend.

The Trunk of Truth

Deep in the forest, standing tall,
A trunk of truth, it knows it all.
With bark that whispers tales of old,
Secrets woven, both brave and bold.

Its roots dig deep, in earth they weave,
Holding stories, hard to believe.
In every ring, a lesson learned,
A history of hearts that burned.

Branches stretching, reaching wide,
Sheltering dreams, where hopes abide.
In canopy's shade, revelations bloom,
Under this tree, there's always room.

The wind through leaves, a soft embrace,
Unveils the truth, a sacred space.
In silence echoes, the world's refrain,
The trunk of truth will always remain.

A Forest of Feelings

In a forest of feelings, shadows dance,
Branches sway in a lover's trance.
Each path diverges with gentle turns,
Where heartbeats echo and passion burns.

Whispers of joy in the rustling leaves,
Branches cradle the secrets we grieve.
With every rustle, emotions swell,
In this embrace, all stories tell.

Stars peek through in the twilight haze,
Guiding souls through the night's maze.
In the silence, a heart may roam,
In the forest's heart, it finds a home.

Through tangled thorns and blossoms bright,
We navigate through wrongs and rights.
A labyrinth of feelings, pure and deep,
In this sacred place, our souls will leap.

Fragrance of the Soul

A scent of warmth fills the air,
Whispers of memories linger there.
Each note a story, sweet and rare,
Fragrance of the soul, beyond compare.

In gardens bright where petals bloom,
Love's gentle touch dispels the doom.
A bouquet woven with joyous threads,
Every fragrance where hope treads.

Through twilight's dusk and morning's light,
Scented dreams take gentle flight.
In every breath, a dance unfolds,
Fragrance of the soul, a tale retold.

In quiet moments, solace found,
With every heartbeat, love is crowned.
The essence of life, a sweet embrace,
Within the soul's fragrance, find your place.

Conversations with the Sky

Beneath the vast, blue sphere,
Whispers dance on gentle breeze,
Clouds drift by with tales to share,
Sunset paints with vibrant ease.

Stars emerge in twilight's song,
Moonlight bathes the world in grace,
Nature hums where hearts belong,
In this vast, celestial space.

Winds converse with leaves on high,
Echoes of a distant past,
Each new day, the sun will rise,
While shadows of the night are cast.

Together, time begins to fade,
In the arms of endless skies,
Every moment softly laid,
In the realm where silence lies.

Blossoming in Silence

In a garden of soft dreams,
Petals open with a sigh,
Every hue holds secret beams,
Painting whispers on the sky.

Gentle breezes carry tales,
Through the branches, love will flow,
Nature's breath in quiet trails,
A serenade for hearts to know.

Roots entwined beneath the ground,
Silent stories intertwine,
In this peace, no discord found,
All unfolds in perfect time.

Blossoms share their silent grace,
In this haven, still and bright,
Every bloom a warm embrace,
Flowering love, pure delight.

Guardians of the Grove

Ancient trees with watchful eyes,
Guard the secrets of the land,
With their roots, they touch the skies,
In stillness, together they stand.

Whispers echo in the shade,
Rustling leaves like voices speak,
In their arms, all fears can fade,
Nature's strength for those who seek.

Beneath the boughs, the earth breathes,
Life unfolds with each new spring,
In their shadows, the heart weaves,
Stories of the souls they bring.

Time stands still in sacred space,
Every moment a soft gift,
Nature's beauty, a warm embrace,
In the grove, the spirits lift.

The Palette of Emotion

Every color tells a tale,
Crimson rage, and azure peace,
On this canvas, brushstrokes sail,
Where feelings blend and never cease.

Amber joys in golden rays,
Shadows fall with shades of grey,
Each hue a song, each stroke a praise,
In the heart's gallery, they play.

Emerald depths of hidden fears,
Violet dreams of worlds unknown,
Every shade holds laughter, tears,
In this art, our truths are shown.

Life, a masterpiece unfolds,
In every stroke, the passions flow,
With every tale that time beholds,
The palette speaks, continues to grow.

Intertwined Histories

In shadows cast by ancient tales,
Echoes of dreams entwined like trails.
Two hearts dance on paths unclear,
Whispers of time, drawing near.

Fragments of stories softly spoken,
Promises made, yet unbroken.
Through fires and storms, we tread,
Holding the past, forging ahead.

Beneath the stars, in night's embrace,
We seek the truth, a sacred space.
Roots that bind, horizons wide,
Interwoven souls, side by side.

History's tapestry, threads in gold,
A journey shared, a bond foretold.
Together we rise, together we fall,
In this dance of life, we answer the call.

Fragments of Bliss

In morning light, the world awakes,
Soft breeze whispers, joy it makes.
Petals fall from blooming trees,
Nature's laughter in the breeze.

Moments captured, brief yet bright,
Stars that twinkle in the night.
Eyes that meet and spark a flame,
Hearts that whisper a secret name.

Raindrops shimmer on thirsty ground,
Melodies of peace abound.
In laughter shared, in silence deep,
Fragments of bliss, forever keep.

As time flows on, we hold these dear,
Every smile, every tear.
In the tapestry of space and time,
We find the rhythm, love's sweet rhyme.

Pilgrimage of the Soul

Step by step on paths unknown,
Seeds of wisdom silently sown.
In the quiet, truths arise,
Guided by the stars in the skies.

Mountains rise and rivers flow,
The heart whispers what we know.
Each stumble teaches us to stand,
Upon this journey, hand in hand.

In valleys low and peaks so high,
We search for meaning, asking why.
Through shadows cast, through light's embrace,
We find our strength, we find our place.

A sacred quest, with every mile,
The spirit's journey, a fleeting smile.
In every heartbeat, every sigh,
The pilgrimage of the soul floats high.

The Symphony of Seasons

Spring awakens with a gentle sigh,
Colors burst under a brightening sky.
Life renews, as blossoms bloom,
Hope reborn from winter's gloom.

Summer dances with vibrant light,
Days stretch long into the night.
Laughter echoes by the shore,
Moments cherished, memories soar.

Autumn whispers with a golden hue,
Leaves falling, painting paths anew.
In the crisp air, a promise made,
Change is constant, never to fade.

Winter blankets all in white,
Stars twinkle in the quiet night.
A time of rest, of reflection's grace,
The seasons turn in soft embrace.

Together they weave a grand refrain,
The cycle of life, joy and pain.
A symphony played by time's sweet hand,
In every heartbeat, a timeless band.

A Garden of Sentiments

In the garden where dreams bloom bright,
Petals whisper tales of delight.
Colors vibrant, hearts entwined,
Each fragrance lingers, love defined.

Beneath the sky, the sun will rise,
Casting shadows, brightening sighs.
Moments cherished, softly sown,
In this space, we are not alone.

Tread lightly on the path of hope,
Each flower teaches us to cope.
A gentle breeze brings forth a song,
In this garden, we all belong.

With each season, emotions flow,
Roots of laughter, seeds we sow.
In the heart of nature's grace,
A sanctuary, our sacred place.

Leaves of Lost Time

Falling softly, memories drift,
Each leaf a moment, a cherished gift.
Whispers of laughter, echoes of tears,
In every fold, a tale appears.

Golden hues of yesterday,
Shimmer in the light of play.
Time wraps gently, a fleeting dance,
Lost in the beauty of happenstance.

Through the rustle, one can hear,
The stories held, both far and near.
Nature's canvas, painted wide,
A tapestry of time, our guide.

In autumn's breath, we find a way,
To hold the past in the light of day.
Leaves may fall, but love remains,
In every heartbeat, joy sustains.

Whispers of Emotions

In the stillness, emotions speak,
Soft as shadows, tender and meek.
A sigh escapes, a heart laid bare,
In gentle echoes, love's sweet air.

Fragrant memories drift and weave,
Through the moments, we dare believe.
Unspoken words, a silent plea,
In every glance, a shared decree.

The pulse of dreams, a quiet hum,
In the night's embrace, we become.
Every heartbeat, a cherished tone,
In whispers deep, we are not alone.

Caught in starlight, shadows sway,
Guided by hope, we find our way.
Each tear, a testament of grace,
In the whispers, we find our place.

Roots of Reflection

Deep beneath where shadows lie,
Roots entangle, reaching high.
In the stillness, thoughts will grow,
Nurtured by time, wisdom flows.

A mirror held to nature's heart,
Revealing truths, a work of art.
Beneath the surface, stories bloom,
In silent echoes, dispelling gloom.

The passage of years, a winding road,
Every step, a gentle load.
Through cracks of doubt, hope finds a way,
In the roots, we learn to stay.

Reflecting on the lives we've led,
From the past, our spirits fed.
In the dance of shadows and light,
Roots of reflection guide our flight.

Mornings of Reflection

Gentle light creeps through the shade,
Whispers of dreams, softly laid.
Thoughts awaken with the dawn,
In this moment, life feels drawn.

Crickets hush, the world stands still,
A quiet heart begins to fill.
Nature speaks in tranquil tones,
In silence, truth's grace is shown.

Each breath taken, a canvas wide,
Memories dance, nowhere to hide.
With each sip of morning air,
Time unfolds, a treasure rare.

As shadows stretch, the sun takes flight,
Courage grows to face the light.
With every thought, a path we pave,
In mornings calm, we learn to brave.

The Weight of Silence

In stillness lies a heavy grace,
Echoes linger in this space.
Unspoken words upon the air,
A haunting truth we often bear.

Eyes meet softly, hearts collide,
In quiet moments, pain can hide.
The weight we carry, a solemn load,
A tale of sorrow, softly flowed.

Yet in this hush, a beauty grows,
Compassion blooms where silence flows.
Together, we learn to understand,
The bonds that break, and those that stand.

With every pause, a chance to heal,
To acknowledge what we feel.
In silence, strength begins to thrive,
As we embrace, we come alive.

Celestial Canopy

Beneath the stars, a world unfolds,
Whispers of tales, ancient and bold.
The moon, a guardian in the night,
Guides our hearts with silver light.

Constellations dance in the sky,
Mapping dreams as they drift by.
In the vast expanse, we find our place,
Lost in wonder, time leaves no trace.

The universe sings in shimmering hues,
A cosmic symphony, a gentle muse.
We reach for the heavens, hope our guide,
In this celestial embrace, we confide.

With each breath, the cosmos we feel,
Intertwined threads that softly heal.
In the night's embrace, we find our way,
Under the stars, forever we stay.

Stories held in Wood

In each grain runs history deep,
Silent secrets that trees keep.
Knots and rings tell of years gone by,
Life's journey wrapped in wood's embrace,

Whispers rustle through the leaves,
Tales of nature, as it weaves.
From forest floor to lofty height,
Every branch holds memories bright.

A childhood swing, a lover's place,
Marks of time we can't erase.
In wooden frames, our joys reside,
Stories linger, hopes abide.

As we carve our names and dreams,
Into this wood, forever gleams.
For every heart, a tale to share,
In stories held, we find our care.

Tapestry of Memories

Threads of colors weave so bright,
In the fabric of the night.
Stories whispered, shadows cast,
In the tapestry of the past.

Moments linger, softly spun,
Echoes of laughter, shadows run.
Each stitch a tale of who we've been,
In the heart where love is seen.

Faded pictures, crumpled dreams,
Life is more than what it seems.
Every memory a crucial part,
Sewn together, soul and heart.

Time unravels but does not fray,
We cherish what will not decay.
Stitched forever, near and far,
In our minds, we keep who we are.

Twilight under the Leaves

Twilight dances, shadows play,
Leaves whisper secrets, soft decay.
Golden rays start to wane,
Nature sighs, calls us again.

Crickets sing their evening song,
As twilight lingers, sweet and long.
A breeze carries the scent of night,
Stars awaken, one by one in sight.

Under the canopy, worlds collide,
In this moment, we can hide.
With the dusk, our worries fade,
In the twilight's gentle shade.

Memories blossom in fading light,
Hearts unite in the still of night.
Together beneath the vast sky,
Twilight wraps us, you and I.

The Embrace of Earth

In the cradle of grass, we lie,
The earth holds us, whispers nigh.
Roots dig deep, a sacred bond,
Through solid ground, we are beyond.

Mountains rise, clouds hover low,
In nature's arms, our spirits grow.
From the soil, strength we find,
Embraced by earth, heart, and mind.

Seasons change with a gentle flow,
In every cycle, life will show.
The rhythm of nature, rich and vast,
In every breath, we are steadfast.

Together we flourish, hand in hand,
In the embrace of this great land.
Forever anchored, forever free,
In the heart of earth, we'll always be.

Roots in the Soul

Deep in the earth, our roots entwine,
Drawing strength from the divine.
Life's harsh trials, we endure,
With roots in the soul, we stand secure.

Through storms and drought, we find our way,
In the darkest nights, we seek the day.
With each challenge, we grow bold,
Roots in the soul, stories told.

Branches stretch, reach for the sky,
But deep below, our spirits lie.
In the quiet, wisdom flows,
From the depths, true strength grows.

Connected to all, a sacred thread,
By love and hope, we are fed.
Roots in the soul, forever tied,
In this journey, we will abide.

Shadows Under the Canopy

Beneath the leaves, whispers play,
Softly dancing, light and gray.
Mysteries hide in nature's folds,
Secrets shared, silently told.

Cool the air, the world holds breath,
Among the trees, we find our myths.
Shadows stretch, whisper and tease,
In the quiet, hearts find ease.

Branches sway with stories old,
Symbols carved, a tale unfolds.
Every rustle, a gentle song,
In this haven, we belong.

Footsteps trace the forest floor,
Echoes linger, wanting more.
In the dusk, the shadows blend,
Under the canopy, we mend.

Whispering Winds of Change

Through the trees, the breezes sigh,
Carrying dreams that float on by.
Each soft gust, a secret shared,
A call to arms, if one has dared.

Days may shift like shifting sand,
New horizons, futures planned.
With every gust, our hopes take flight,
Chasing shadows, seeking light.

Colors swirl in vibrant dance,
A chance to grow, a brand-new chance.
Feel the pulse of change awake,
As the world's rhythms start to shake.

In this moment, we can rise,
Embrace the change, reach for the skies.
With whispering winds, we'll find our way,
Every heartbeat, a new day.

Boughs of Belonging

Under the boughs, we stand so close,
In this shelter, we are chose.
Roots entwined like fingers clasped,
In this bond, so tightly grasped.

Branches held against the sky,
Where dreams are born, we learn to fly.
Every leaf tells tales of old,
In the warmth, we feel consoled.

Seasons shift, yet we remain,
Along this path, through joy and pain.
Among the roots, the love runs deep,
In this embrace, our hearts can leap.

Here in nature, our spirits blend,
Among the boughs, we find our friends.
Together strong, we lift each other,
In the warmth, we find our mother.

The Symphony of Seasons

Spring awakens with colors bright,
Life anew in morning light.
Flowers bloom, a sweet embrace,
Nature's canvas, filled with grace.

Summer's laughter fills the air,
Golden rays for those who dare.
In the heat, the world ignites,
Joy abounds in shining sights.

Autumn whispers a soft goodbye,
Leaves of gold begin to fly.
The chill arrives, a crisp refrain,
Nature's beauty, a sweet pain.

Winter blankets all in white,
Stars above shine through the night.
Quiet moments, peace descends,
In this stillness, magic bends.

Whispers of the Heartwood

In the grove where silence breathes,
Whispers dance on gentle leaves.
Soft shadows cast by towering trees,
Ancient tales carried on the breeze.

Branches bend with secrets kept,
Underneath, the sun has wept.
In the stillness, soft hearts blend,
Echoes of love that never end.

Roots entwined beneath the ground,
In the darkness, hope is found.
Each heartbeat like a drum,
Telling stories as they come.

So listen close, let silence start,
For in the woods, lives the heart.
Whispers linger, never part,
In the shadows, find your heart.

Emotions Like Leaves

Emotions flutter with the breeze,
Dancing lightly from the trees.
Golden hues in autumn's glow,
Whispers of the love we know.

Fallen leaves, a soft embrace,
Memories time cannot erase.
In their crunch, a story shared,
Understanding, always bared.

Through each season, colors change,
Feelings shift, the world's so strange.
But beneath the changing skies,
Each heart sings, and never lies.

Like leaves in wind, we sway and spin,
Finding comfort from within.
Connected by the sturdy boughs,
Emotions strong, in silence, vow.

Branches of Sentiment

Branches reach for skies so wide,
Carrying whispers, hearts inside.
Each twist tells of love and pain,
Nature's mirror, bright and plain.

Hopes and dreams on darts of light,
Dancing gently through the night.
In the shadows, truth unfurls,
Woven deep in worldly whirls.

As they grow, we feel the strain,
Tangled roots of joy and bane.
Yet through storms, they stand so bold,
Stories of the brave retold.

With every branch, a choice bestowed,
A path revealed, a longing flowed.
In this forest, life's embrace,
Branches of love, our sacred space.

Roots of Reflection

Roots extend where shadows lie,
Deep beneath the vast blue sky.
In the stillness, truths align,
Gathered wisdom, pure and fine.

Each tendril grips the earth so firm,
In soft whispers, thoughts affirm.
Through time's flow, our stories blend,
In silent strength, connections mend.

With every heartbeat, memories rise,
In the quiet, wisdom lies.
Reflecting all that came before,
Roots of life, a steady core.

Beneath us, ancient echoes call,
Binding us within their thrall.
In this grounding, we find grace,
Roots of reflection, our safe space.

Echoing Heartbeats

In the stillness of the night,
I hear whispers of the past,
Each heartbeat shares a secret,
In shadows that forever cast.

Moments dance like fireflies,
Flickering in twilight's gleam,
Every pulse a memory,
Woven in a fragile dream.

Echoes linger in the air,
Soft reminders of our bond,
Hearts entwined in rhythm's grace,
A melody that goes beyond.

In this symphony of souls,
We find solace in the night,
Echoing heartbeats hold us close,
In the dark, we find our light.

The Dance of Time

Ticking clocks and fleeting days,
Each moment slips away,
A ballet of the hours,
In a delicate display.

Seasons swirl in vibrant hues,
Leaves fall soft like whispered sighs,
Time pirouettes in circles,
Beneath the vast, unfolding skies.

With every tick, a story told,
Stories of love, of loss, of grace,
A dance where memories unfold,
In life's unhurried pace.

Twilight breathes the end of day,
As stars emerge, they softly chime,
In the cosmic waltz we sway,
Forever lost in the dance of time.

Nurturing the Quiet

In the hush of morning light,
Soft whispers fill the air,
Nature cradles every sound,
In a calm and tender care.

Beneath the trees, shadows lay,
Nature's quilt, a gentle spread,
Each breeze carries dreams anew,
In the silence, words unsaid.

Time stands still in quietude,
Peace envelops every spark,
Nurturing hearts out of sight,
In the stillness, love ignites.

Let the world fade into calm,
As we embrace the serene,
In the nurturing of quiet,
Life's beauty, ever keen.

Remnants of Raindrops

When the storm has come and gone,
Puddles gleam like shards of glass,
Each raindrop holds a world inside,
Reflections of the moments past.

Air is sweet with earth's perfume,
Colors bright and spirits rise,
Nature sings a soft refrain,
Underneath the painted skies.

With every drop that falls to ground,
Echoes of the thunder fade,
Memories of clouds unwind,
In the silence, joy is made.

So let the remnants linger on,
A tapestry of light and shade,
For in each raindrop's gentle fall,
Life's essence is displayed.

Softening Shadows

In the dusk, shadows fade,
Whispers of dreams softly made.
The world dims a tender hue,
As I wander, lost in you.

Misty corners hold the light,
Gentle calm transforms the night.
Each step veils what's left behind,
In softening shadows, hearts unwind.

Silent moments breathe anew,
Rustling leaves, a dance to view.
Embraced by a twilight gray,
Where all worries drift away.

Together we'll chase the stars,
Nothing fragments, no more scars.
In shadows deep, we'll always stay,
Softening with the close of day.

Whirlwind Revelations

Caught in the spin of life,
Truths arise amidst the strife.
Thoughts collide, a storm's embrace,
Whispers echo, filling space.

Fleeting moments twist and weave,
Lessons learned, we dare believe.
In the chaos, clarity,
Sparks ignite creativity.

Turbulence carries us along,
Voices rise in vibrant song.
Together we shall weave delight,
Through rapid storms, find our light.

With every twist, a chance to grow,
In the whirlwind, seeds we sow.
Embrace the dance, let it flow,
Whirlwind truths begin to glow.

Hidden Treasures Within

In the quiet of the mind,
Lost echoes are hard to find.
But beneath the surface lies,
Beauty clad in great disguise.

Layers rich, like ancient clay,
Form the paths we walk each day.
Uncovering the gems of soul,
Chasing glimpses, feeling whole.

With every heartbeat, secrets call,
In shadowed corners, treasures fall.
Dare to seek the light inside,
Where hidden wonders choose to bide.

From depths of silence, truths arise,
Transforming tears into the prize.
Within our hearts, vast worlds awake,
Hidden treasures we will take.

A Journey through Colors

On the path of vivid dreams,
Life unfolds in endless beams.
Every hue, a step to take,
In this journey, hearts awake.

Amber sunsets, golden dusk,
Petals fresh with fragrant musk.
Cerulean skies hold the day,
In colors bright, we drift away.

Emerald forests call the brave,
Mystic hues in waters wave.
Colors shimmer, spirits rise,
Painting life beneath the skies.

Each shade tells a story bold,
In every heart, a tale unfolds.
Together we will roam anew,
In a journey through vibrant hues.

Growth through Storms

In the heart of thunder's roar,
Roots dig deeper, seeking more.
Strengthened by the wildest night,
Emerging bold, embracing light.

Winds may bend the fragile trees,
Yet they stand with sturdy ease.
Growth arises from the fray,
Blooming brighter day by day.

Raindrops wash away the fear,
Nurture whispers, loud and clear.
In the chaos, beauty grows,
Resilience through each wind that blows.

Through the tempest, lessons learned,
In each struggle, hope is earned.
From the storm, a vision grand,
Nature's wonders, hand in hand.

Boughs of Belief

Underneath the sky so wide,
Branches stretch, they do not hide.
Each leaf holds a whispered prayer,
Faith in roots that intertwine.

In the silence, strength is found,
Winds may howl, but won't confound.
Hope rises like the morning sun,
Together we shall overcome.

Boughs of belief, strong and true,
Cherished dreams in every hue.
With each season, we unite,
Through the darkness, we find light.

In the shade, we share our trust,
Nurtured by the bonds of us.
Together strong, forever bound,
In the forest, love is found.

The Rhythm of Nature

Softly beats the heart of earth,
Every creature knows its worth.
Seasons flow like waves in time,
Nature sings her perfect rhyme.

Whispers dance through rustling leaves,
Sunlight filters, softly weaves.
In the streams, the flow remains,
Life's pulse moves through joys and pains.

Mountains rise, then gently fall,
Echoes of the ancient call.
Stars align in night's embrace,
In each moment, find your place.

Rhythm found in every breeze,
Harmony in swaying trees.
With each step, we join the song,
Moving forward, where we belong.

Kaleidoscope of Hues

Colors burst with vibrant cheer,
Each shade tells a story clear.
In the garden, life's parade,
Nature's brush, a grand charade.

Petals dance in morning light,
Every glance, a pure delight.
Swirling patterns, bright and bold,
Secrets of the earth retold.

From the dusk to dawn's embrace,
Spectrum paints a sacred space.
In the twilight, shades collide,
Magic flows, we stand beside.

Kaleidoscope of dreams awakes,
Beauty found in all it makes.
In each color, life redeems,
Together weaving our shared dreams.

Sparrows and Secrets

In the hush of early morn,
Sparrows chirp their gentle song.
Secrets hidden in soft wings,
Whispers of where they belong.

They flit through branches green and tall,
Dancing with the breeze at play.
Each flutter holds a fleeting tale,
Of life in shades of gray.

Beneath the boughs, the world awakes,
Soft sunbeams kiss the dew-kissed ground.
Sparrows spin their stories small,
In every chirp, a note profound.

Under skies both blue and gray,
They weave their paths with endless cheer.
For in their flight, a secret lives,
Of hope and dreams, forever near.

The Art of Letting Go

Fingers release the autumn leaves,
Drifting softly to the ground.
The art of letting go unfolds,
In every rustle, wisdom found.

Moments cherished, yet they fade,
Like shadows cast at end of day.
Each breath a step, a choice to make,
To dance with change, come what may.

Memories held like fragile glass,
Reflecting joy, the bittersweet.
In letting go, we find our peace,
A melody, a steady beat.

With open hearts, we learn to trust,
To fall like leaves and rise anew.
The art of letting go reveals,
A world of light, waiting for you.

Bursting with Possibility

In the garden, seeds lay deep,
Dreams of flowers yet to bloom.
With every raindrop, life awakes,
Bursting forth from darkened tombs.

Sunlight bathes the world in gold,
Nurturing hopes, so bold and bright.
Each stir of root, a new embrace,
Of possibilities taking flight.

Petals twirl in vibrant hues,
Painting joy on nature's stage.
With every breeze, new stories spin,
A dance of life, forever sage.

Bursting forth, the earth will sing,
A symphony of growth and grace.
In every bud, a promise lies,
Of beauty found in every place.

Whims of the Wind

The wind whispers secrets low,
Twisting tales through trees so tall.
It carries dreams on gentle breath,
A sighing, breezy call.

It plays with leaves in playful spurts,
Dancing through the autumn chill.
With every gust, a story stirs,
Nature's heart, a restless thrill.

Whims of the wind, both fierce and sweet,
Guide the ships across the sea.
It lifts the kites and stirs the clouds,
A timeless, wandering decree.

So let it sweep you in its arms,
And take you where the wild things roam.
For in the wind, we find our place,
A journey home, a glimpse of home.

Milton Keynes UK
Ingram Content Group UK Ltd.
UKHW020151291024
450401UK00007B/108

9 789916 889268